Original title: Celestial Visions

Author: Aron Pilviste
Editor: Jessica Elisabeth Luik
ISBN 978-9916-39-963-7

Celestial Visions

Aron Pilviste

Starry Wanderlust

Beneath the velvet sky at night,
I chase the stars, a wondrous flight,
Their whispers draw me far and near,
To realms unseen, both bright and clear.

By light of moon, my path adorned,
Through cosmic seas where dreams are born,
The constellations guide my way,
In silent songs they softly sway.

I dance with shadows, dark and deep,
Through boundless night where secrets sleep,
In every sparkle, tales untold,
Of ancient hearts and spirits bold.

Among the galaxies so wide,
I seek the truths that stars confide,
Their glowing hints of love and fate,
In timeless realms, I contemplate.

Let cosmos be my boundless guide,
In starry realms I've nothing to hide,
For in the night, I find my worth,
A wanderer of sky and earth.

Planetary Poetry

In orbit's gentle dance, we twirl
Around a sun, our golden pearl
With cosmic rhythms, we align
In stellar hugs, so divine

Moonlit whispers through the night
Stars in galaxies ignite
Each planet's tale, softly spoke
In time's embrace, ev'ry yoke

Meteors blaze in midnight skies
Wishes born where comet dies
Nebulae, in hues cascade
In astral art, dreams are made

Cosmos's tune, a symphony
Notes of worlds in harmony
In space's expanse, we belong
To planetary poetry, we song

Universal Cascades

Rivers of time in endless flow
Across the universe, they go
From birth of stars to twilight's shade
In cosmic webs, their paths are laid

Light speed dance through darkened seas
Nebulae in silent pleas
Galaxies in whirlpools spin
In universal cascades, we begin

Quasars pulse in rhythmic beat
Echoes of the cosmos greet
Black holes whisper voids so deep
Quintessence, the world to keep

Stardust sprinkled in the air
Glimmers caught in twilight fair
In this cosmic masquerade
Universal secrets fade

Celestial Serenades

Beneath the stars, a melody
Infinite in harmony
Planets hum in endless rhyme
In celestial moments, time

Solar winds through skies so vast
Singing tales of aeons past
Orbs of light in silent aid
Join the celestial serenade

Auroras paint the polar skies
Symphonies of light arise
Echoes in the firmament
In stardust whispers, we are lent

Across the void, a chorus rings
Of galaxies and distant things
In this space, our hearts pervade
With celestial serenades

Infinite Nightfall

As night descends with velvet cloak
Stars awake, their light they stoke
Underneath this twilight sprawl
We embrace infinite nightfall

Whispers of the moonlight stream
Guiding us through quiet dream
Cosmic shadows softly call
In the arms of night we fall

Galaxy's kiss, a sweet caress
In the dark, we find our rest
In the deep, where visions dwell
Infinite tales, stars do tell

Veil of night in silver sheen
Cosmic dance in midnight's scene
In this hush, where dreams enthrall
We embrace infinite nightfall

Heavens Unveiled

Stars whisper secrets, silent and bright,
Their ancient tales through endless night.
Galaxies spiral in cosmic dance,
Mysteries unveil with every glance.

Auroras paint skies in spectral hues,
Celestial wonders come into view.
Infinite vastness, a boundless stage,
Universe opens, page by page.

Constellations map a stellar lore,
Heavens unveiled, forevermore.
Planets orbit in rhythmic flow,
Eternal grandeur, endless glow.

Transcendent Tides

Oceans breathe with lunar grace,
Waves touch shore in soft embrace.
Tides of time, rise and fall,
Nature's rhythm, heed her call.

Moon's allure, magnet of seas,
Waters dance with gentle ease.
Whispers of the deep, ancient, wise,
Mysteries hidden beneath blue skies.

Harmony flows where currents meet,
Transcendent tides, a heartbeat.
Cycles woven, life's grand thread,
In ocean's depths, all is said.

Eclipse of Dreams

Shadows merge with light's soft gleam,
In twilight's arms, we dare to dream.
Moon and sun in cosmic flight,
Embrace the darkness, kiss the light.

Stars burn bright in midnight skies,
Eclipses create night's surprise.
Dreams emerge in shadow's sway,
Night and day in soft array.

Veils of sleep, realms unknown,
In dreams, we find seeds flown.
Eclipse of dreams, night's grand flight,
Minds awaken to endless light.

Meteors in Motion

Blazing trails light the starlit dome,
Meteors streak, far from home.
Night's canvas touched by fire's might,
A fleeting dance in darkened night.

Cosmic stones, ancient and old,
Burn through skies with stories told.
Showers of light in silent fall,
Witness the wonder, standing tall.

Heavens sigh with burning praise,
Meteors in motion, astral blaze.
Fleeting moments, cosmic tide,
In their glow, our dreams confide.

Nebulae Narratives

In the vast ethereal sprawl,
Where colored clouds gently call,
Nebulae weave stories long,
In whispers of a cosmic song.

Stars are born and fade away,
In their bosom, light will play,
Tales of time and space untold,
In their hues, mysteries unfold.

Galaxies in grand parade,
Through their veils, eternities fade,
Darkness dances with the light,
In this endless, silent night.

Cosmic Ballet

Spirals twirl in astral grace,
Celestial bodies interlace,
In the void, they write their fate,
Every star a dancer's mate.

Planets waltz in rhythmic flow,
Round their suns they shyly go,
Comets dip with icy flair,
Trailing streaks of silver hair.

Asteroids in rumbles spin,
Rocking out in cosmic din,
While nebulae in pastel hues,
Set the stage, diffuse the clues.

Lunar Lanterns

Silent moon with lantern bright,
Glowing in the velvet night,
Casting shadows, birthing dreams,
Midst the starry, silver beams.

Craters mark your ancient face,
Stories told in silent grace,
Tides you pull with gentle force,
Guiding sailors in their course.

Phases wax and wane with time,
Luminous in quiet rhyme,
Mysteries in every phase,
Drawing eyes with endless gaze.

Astral Reverie

In the stillness of the night,
Hearts ascend to wondrous heights,
Dreams on cosmic currents sail,
In the starry, twinkling veil.

Galaxies like gemstones shine,
Casting light on dreams divine,
Nebulae with misty glow,
Whisper secrets we can't know.

Planets hum in low bass tone,
Each in orbit, not alone,
Stars as notes in night's refrain,
Sing a song that's never plain.

Astral Promises

In realms where comets blaze and glide,
Dreams weave through the cosmic tide.
Astral winds whisper secrets sweet,
Promises of stars that never deplete.

Galaxies swirl in a timeless waltz,
Echoing ancient, forgotten calls.
In night's embrace, hearts ignite,
Seeking promises in celestial light.

Nebulae paint the sky with hues,
A canvas bright, where colors fuse.
Infinite journeys await our gaze,
In the astral night's enigmatic maze.

Lunar Echoes

Silver beams through velvet skies,
Whisper tales of lullabies.
Lunar echoes softly croon,
Underneath the watchful moon.

In craters deep, old shadows dwell,
Secrets they would never tell.
Night's serenity soothes the land,
Guided by the moon's gentle hand.

Reflections in the midnight stream,
Chase the whispers of a dream.
Under Luna's tender glow,
Echoes of peace continue to flow.

Galaxy's Serenade

Stars align in cosmic dance,
Filling night with mystic chants.
Galactic choirs softly play,
Tunes of worlds so far away.

Nebulae pulse with vibrant light,
Composing serenades of night.
Planets whirl in rhythmic time,
Spinning through a silent rhyme.

Celestial melodies intertwine,
In the depths where starlight shines.
Harmony of the vast unknown,
In Galaxy's serenade, dreams are sown.

Stellar Reflections

In the quiet of the night's expanse,
Stars reflect in a cosmic trance.
Their light travels from times of yore,
Illuminating dreams galore.

Constellations map the skies,
Mirroring ancient, watchful eyes.
Glistening paths of endless night,
Reflecting wisdom, pure and bright.

Celestial mirrors in the sky,
Hold the truths we can't deny.
In stellar depths, reflections clear,
Understanding dawns, ever near.

Stellar Dreams

In the quiet of the night,
Diamonds glimmer from afar.
Whispers of celestial light,
Guide me towards a wishing star.

Through the cosmic waves I glide,
In the vast, unending sea.
With the universe as my guide,
Bound by dreams that set me free.

Nebulas of vibrant hue,
Paint the canvas of my mind.
Promise skies of endless blue,
Where endless aspirations find.

Nocturnal Symphony

Moonlight serenades the glen,
Softly humming ancient tunes.
Nature's choir joins again,
Beneath the watchful silver moon.

Crickets chant their evening hymn,
Owls echo through the trees.
Each note on the nocturnal whim,
Weaves the night in symphonies.

Stars as silent spectators,
Glisten in their astral seats.
Universe, the grand creator,
Of melodies the night completes.

Ethereal Skies

Above the earthly bounds we fly,
In dreams where heavens softly call.
Ethereal wonders paint the sky,
In hues that drape like a gentle shawl.

Beyond the realm of daily woes,
We soar to realms of light and grace.
Where every star in silence glows,
A beacon in the endless space.

Clouds of silver, clouds of gold,
Drift upon celestial streams.
In the skies, tales of old,
Whisper through our hopeful dreams.

Galactic Whispers

In the silent cosmic night,
Galaxies share their ancient lore.
From the distant points of light,
Whispers that the stars implore.

Planets spin their silent tale,
Around suns that brightly burn.
Through the void, on stardust trails,
The secrets of the past we learn.

Constellations softly speak,
Of wonders that they once have known.
In their whispers, mysteries seep,
In the vast, galactic lone.

Galactic Ballet

In the depths of the void, where silence holds sway,
Stars waltz together in a celestial ballet.
Nebulae swirl in a hypnotic dance,
While comets twirl in an astral trance.

Through cosmic corridors they glide so light,
Eclipsed by the shadows of eternal night.
Galaxies pirouette in a delicate spin,
Their gravitational embrace, where stars begin.

Soft whispers of stardust fill the air,
In this ageless theater, without despair.
Planets revolve in rhythmic delight,
Bathed in the darkness of infinite night.

Ethereal Galaxies

Beyond the horizon of mortal gaze,
Lie ethereal galaxies, in their endless maze.
Streams of light weave through the dark,
Leaving trails of radiance, a cosmic arc.

Milky rivers and luminescent tides,
Flow through the heavens in silent strides.
Each constellation, a story untold,
Written in the fabric of starry gold.

Dreams of the ancients ride on beams,
Emanating from galaxies, casting gleams.
Ethereal beauty, boundless and vast,
A testament to a cosmos that's unsurpassed.

Comet's Crescendo

A comet streaks through the night so grand,
A luminous dagger in the celestial sand.
Its icy heart burns with a fiery glow,
As it carves its mark in the cosmic show.

Trailing a veil of sparkling light,
It soars through the endless night.
A crescendo of brightness, fierce and swift,
An ephemeral gift, a starry rift.

In its wake, silence follows tight,
As it vanishes, a whisper in the night.
But for those who watched its fleeting flare,
A memory etched in the astral air.

Rays of the Quasar

Far beyond where time unravels slow,
Lie the quasar beams, in resplendent glow.
Pulses of light from an ancient core,
Illuminating the cosmos, forevermore.

Every photon, a messenger of might,
Carrying secrets of creation's light.
Their paths traverse the void so pure,
Marking trails in the vastness obscure.

Rays of wonder, boundless and free,
Echoes of eternity, across the galaxy.
The quasar sings its cosmic song,
In the symphony where we all belong.

Phantom Planets

In the silent night they glide
Across the darkest space
Eclipsing stars they often hide
In their ghostly, vagrant race

Nebulas shiver in gentle fright
To feel their phantom flight
Invisible to every light
Yet burning oh so bright

Their trails a shadow's trace
In endless, boundless grace
The cosmic ether they embrace
In their spectral, silent chase

Galaxies whisper secrets deep
Of planets lost in sleep
In the void where they creep
Eternal solitude to keep

Astral silence, voids so vast
Through the ages' quiet blast
In their paths, the echoes cast
Phantom planets from the past

Time's Telescope

Through the lens of ages past
Glimpse worlds of ancient cast
Where moments faded fast
Yet memories ever last

Stardust trails in golden glow
Mark the epochs' ebb and flow
Galaxies in cosmic show
In time's ever-present flow

Idea's born to light and fade
In stars that our eyes bade
By truth and myth arrayed
In the particles they played

Black holes whisper silent lore
Chronicles of cosmic roar
Within the silent core
Of time's uncharted shore

Through time's telescope we peer
Into futures bright and clear
Constant as each passing year
Each moment, held so dear

Event Horizon Echoes

In the black hole's shadowed rim
Light's final, fleeting whim
Where stars to darkness dim
Begins the cosmic hymn

Echoes from the event horizon
Secrets that the void confides in
Whispers with gravity's rising
In space-time distorting and surprising

Atoms churn in silent storm
Gravity in unending form
In the void becoming warm
Particles in cosmic norm

Light engulfs and winds like thread
Around the singularity spread
Silent as the twilight dread
Where even photons tread

Mysteries in the cosmic fold
Stories of the universe told
Echoes from a distance old
In horizons dark and cold

Intergalactic Symphony

Across the void a symphony
Played by cosmic harmony
Stars and planets in melody
In the interstellar sea

Galactic clusters resonate
With tunes the nebula create
Harmonic waves that venerate
The universe's grand estate

Pulsars beat their rhythmic dance
In the deep, entrancing trance
Galaxies whirl in cosmic chance
In time's eternal expanse

Comets blaze with fervent fire
In melodies that never tire
Celestial choirs that inspire
The music of the cosmic lyre

The cosmos hums in grand array
In an intergalactic ballet
Symphonies of light and sway
In the night's vast display

Cosmos Chronicles

In the vast expanse of night,
Stars emerge, a gentle flight,
Whispers of ancient lore,
Echo through space, evermore.

Galaxies in spiral dance,
Nebulas in vivid trance,
Celestial tales unfold,
As the universe grows old.

Planets in their orbits swing,
Moons around them gently cling,
Comets blaze their fiery trails,
Leaving cosmic, sparkling tales.

Black holes with their secret ways,
Warping time, distorting days,
Mysteries in endless tide,
In dark matter they confide.

Constellations, stories weave,
In the sky, their marks they leave,
Journey through this cosmic sea,
Chronicles of infinity.

Infinity's Canvas

On the canvas of the night,
Drawn by stars, a surging light,
Patterns form in twilight's hue,
In the heavens, shades of blue.

Nebulas in colors rare,
Swirling with celestial flair,
Brushstrokes of the cosmic hand,
Painting worlds of wonder grand.

Comets streak with fiery grace,
Across the boundless space,
Leaving trails of glowing fire,
Sparks of dreams and hearts' desire.

Galaxies in arcs align,
Strokes defining space and time,
Woven in the night's embrace,
Infinite in form and place.

Through the void where silence speaks,
Where the vast unknown peeks,
Artistry in cosmic sprawl,
Infinity reveals its all.

Quantum Quests

Quantum realms where shadows play,
In the laws of night and day,
Particles in dance they twirl,
Mysteries of the micro world.

Waves and dots, a dual guise,
Secrets held in tangled ties,
Entanglement in space and time,
Quantum's silent, rhythmic rhyme.

Probabilities unfold,
Stories waiting to be told,
Through the slits of ancient light,
Parallel paths, a hidden sight.

Superposition's stealthy mask,
Answers lie in every ask,
Universe of smallest might,
Reveals its wonders in the night.

Subatomic dreams converge,
In a dance, they weave and merge,
Quests of quantum, vast and sly,
In the realms where atoms fly.

Stardust Symphony

Whispers in the cosmic wind,
Notes of stars and tales twinned,
Harmony in stellar light,
Symphony through endless night.

Melody of planets spin,
Echoes of what once has been,
Harmony in orbits prime,
Cosmic rhythm, boundless time.

Comets blaze with fiery cries,
Singing through the star-lit skies,
Brilliant chords of ancient lore,
Echoing forevermore.

Black holes hum in deepest tones,
Gravity's soft undertones,
Songs of space and time entwined,
In the vastness, secrets find.

Stars compose with fiery breath,
Symphony that conquers death,
Celestial voices rise above,
In the universe's love.

Galaxies Awaken

In the hush of twilight's gleam,
Galaxies awaken from their dream.
Spirals of stars begin to twirl,
Mysteries unfold as night unfurls.

Cosmic wonders stretch afar,
Enchanting every wandering star.
Nebulas in shades of blue,
Painting skies with celestial hue.

Planets dance in silent grace,
Across the boundless, dark embrace.
Whispers of ancient light remain,
Echoes of a different plane.

Comets streak through endless night,
Illuminating paths of light.
Constellations, bright and free,
Weave a timeless tapestry.

Galaxies awaken, timeless and vast,
Windows to a forgotten past.
In their depths, secrets lay,
Stories told in light's array.

Orion's Odyssey

Orion strides with mighty bow,
Across the sky in endless glow.
Hunter of the starry night,
Guiding ships with steadfast light.

Betelgeuse and Rigel shine,
Marking paths through space and time.
The sword he carries, glittering bright,
Pierces through the cosmic night.

Journey through the Milky Way,
Where stars in vivid colors play.
Myths and legends intertwine,
In the vast celestial design.

Nebulae of hues so grand,
Orion's sight, a guiding hand.
Through stardust realms he makes his flight,
Guardian of the endless night.

Odyssey of stars and dreams,
In the dark, his presence gleams.
Orion's journey, bold and free,
Eternal in the galaxy.

Heavenly Journeys

Heavenly journeys through the night,
With stars as guides and moon as light.
Wandering through the cosmic sea,
Boundless realms of mystery.

Planets whisper tales untold,
Of adventures brave and bold.
Through celestial paths we soar,
Exploring wonders, searching more.

Milky Way streams silver bright,
Lighting paths of endless height.
Across the universe so wide,
On stardust trails we silently glide.

Galactic winds, with gentle sigh,
Carrying dreams beyond the sky.
Heavenly bodies, one by one,
Join the voyage, now begun.

In the realms of endless night,
Heavenly journeys take their flight.
Mysteries revealed in turns,
As each new corner of space we learn.

Meteor Mysteries

Meteors streak across the sky,
Burning bright as they fly by.
Glimmers of an ancient past,
Moments fleeting, yet they last.

Silent whispers through the air,
Mysteries beyond compare.
Sparks that light the velvet dome,
Each a traveler far from home.

Asteroids and comets play,
In the dark, they find their way.
Glistening trails mark their flight,
Jewels in the endless night.

Crashing through the void so grand,
Mysteries in every strand.
Meteor showers, bright and clear,
Illuminating night sincere.

Mysteries of meteors unfold,
Tales in stardust, bright and bold.
Every flash and fiery flight,
A secret of the sky's delight.

Pulsar's Pulse

A heartbeat in the silent night,
Cosmic echoes pure and bright,
Through the void its rhythms kite,
An ancient tale of endless flight.

Starlit whispers weave and mend,
Galactic bounds they transcend,
In their blaze, we comprehend,
The lore of time they extend.

At the dusk of distant space,
Diamonds cast in darkened lace,
Orbit still in timeless chase,
Pulsar's pulse, a steady grace.

Interstellar beacons gleam,
Guiding dreams in astral stream,
In the throes of cosmic dream,
Light eternal, so supreme.

Silent reverie unfurls,
Spinning in celestial whirls,
Through the night it softly twirls,
In the heart, forever swirls.

Vanishing Vortex

In the void where shadows spin,
A whisper beckons from within,
Twilight's dance on velvet skin,
Where cosmic dreams begin.

Whirling winds of mystic dust,
Timeless voids of shadowed lust,
Through the realms of stars and rust,
Wonders there we trust.

Galaxies in spirals tight,
Drawn towards an endless night,
Where the dark devours light,
Insatiable, infinite sight.

In the chasm's silent call,
Stars and hopes begin to fall,
Vanishing, where none enthrall,
Lost within the vortex thrall.

Eternal sway of unseen force,
Guiding through an unknown course,
In its grip, a silent source,
Cosmic tides in endless morse.

Gravity's Grace

In the silence of the skies,
Where the timeless beauty lies,
Inward pulls of cosmic ties,
Gravity's grace never denies.

Stars are held in tender clasp,
Galaxies in endless grasp,
Through the void, in space they rasp,
Bound by an unseen gasp.

Planets dance in steady line,
Round the suns they intertwine,
Orbits held by force divine,
Songs of spheres and time combine.

In the vast expanse, they flow,
Weights unseen, yet all bestow,
Gravity's gentle ebb and tow,
Holds the cosmos in its glow.

Mystic threads of space and time,
Woven by an unseen rhyme,
In its calm, chaotic prime,
Gravity's grace, forever sublime.

Craters of Delight

On the moon's pale, cratered face,
Ancient tales in shadows trace,
Whispers of a silent race,
In those valleys vast embrace.

Silver prairies stretch afar,
Twinkling with each distant star,
Echoes of a cosmic scar,
Beauty found where voids are.

Footprints where the dust has lain,
Silent paths in lunar plain,
Memories of joy and pain,
In each crater, wisdom's vein.

Starlit nights with magic filled,
In those heavens, dreams distilled,
Craters where our hopes are willed,
Hearts with wonder softly thrilled.

Eternal twilight's soft caress,
Where the astral spirits bless,
In the craters we confess,
Awestruck by their quiet press.

Orbiting Opus

In silent voids, our hearts align,
On cosmic waves, we intertwine.
Satellites in night's embrace,
We trace the stars, we dare to chase.

Whispers of the moons we hear,
Through nebula and clusters near.
In this dance without a sound,
An opus in the sky unbound.

Galaxies in endless spin,
Where timeless love has always been.
Orbiting, a tale we write,
Under this eternal night.

Through the void, our spirits soar,
Infinity to still explore.
A symphony of dreams and light,
Together, boundless in our flight.

And as we traverse this expanse,
In cosmic waltz, we take our chance.
In celestial harmony,
Our orbiting symphony.

Hubble's Glimpse

A window to the vast afar,
Revealing secrets of a star.
In colors vibrant, hues so bright,
Hubble's gaze, a cosmic sight.

Through time and space, its lens does peer,
Unveiling realms both far and near.
Galaxies in their grand parade,
In hues of blue and crimson shade.

Nebulae in wisps of light,
In darkness bold, so soft, so bright.
A tapestry of time and space,
In Hubble's glimpse, the cosmos trace.

Reflections of the great unknown,
In every frame, a universe shown.
The mysteries of the night unfurled,
In each snapshot, a hidden world.

So let us dream and let us yearn,
Through Hubble's eyes, the stars we learn.
A glimpse of what could always be,
In the infinite tapestry.

Galactic Gazes

Eyes lifted to the midnight sea,
Where stars in silence, whisper free.
With dreams upon the astral beam,
Galactic gazes weave a dream.

Constellations paint the sky,
Stories old that never die.
Through telescopes, our visions stream,
In cosmic spans, our spirits gleam.

Galaxies with gentle grace,
In sparkling clusters, we embrace.
Enchanted by their distant hum,
In starlit awe, our hearts succumb.

Wanderers of the astral plane,
In endless night, our desires reign.
Through celestial tapestries,
We traverse the galaxies.

In unity, we watch and wait,
For cosmic wonders to translate.
Galactic gazes, timeless flight,
Bound by stars and endless night.

Starry Symphony

Above the world in silent grace,
The stars align, in cosmic place.
A symphony so pure and grand,
Unfolds above the twilight land.

Melodies of ancient light,
In whispers soft, so clear, so bright.
The night sky draws us close to hear,
A starry symphony so near.

In constellations, notes do bind,
Orchestrating realms combined.
Celestial chords weave through the dark,
In every star, a silent spark.

Infinite the tune will flow,
Through the heavens, high and low.
Celestial music, pure, unchained,
In every soul, its touch retained.

May we always, as we gaze,
Find harmony in starlit maze.
In the silence of the night,
Hear the starry symphony's plight.

Planetary Portraits

In twilight's gentle, glowing hue,
Planets align in cosmic view.
Spinning in their silent dance,
A symphony of astral chance.

From Mercury's swift, fleeting gleam,
To Neptune's deep, cerulean dream,
Each world paints the endless sky,
Their tales written high and nigh.

Saturn's rings like artist's stroke,
Gaseous worlds in colors soak.
Jupiter's storms forever rage,
A drama on a distant stage.

Mars in red, a dusty plight,
While Venus glows with fiery light.
Earth, our home, so rich and bright,
In the vast celestial night.

Each planet a portrait, a tale to tell,
In the vast darkness, where they dwell.
Connected by gravity's unseen thread,
In the cosmic story, forever spread.

Celestial Silhouettes

Against the canvas of the night,
Silhouettes of stars ignite.
Shadows cast by distant suns,
Timeless, as the river runs.

Nebulae form ghostly shapes,
Woven in the cosmic drapes.
Galaxies in spiraled dance,
Eternal in their vast expanse.

Moons that whisper to the seas,
Orbiting with gentle ease.
Silhouettes on cratered lands,
Carved by the celestial hands.

Asteroids in silent flight,
Marking paths in endless night.
Celestial shadows, bold and free,
Wonders of our galaxy.

Silhouettes in cosmic glow,
Stories of the stars that flow.
In the night sky, quiet yet grand,
Celestial wonders, finely planned.

Cosmos Chronicles

In the chronicles of time and space,
Eons pass without a trace.
Stars are born and then they die,
Whispers of the cosmic sigh.

Galaxies in clusters twirl,
In a vast and endless swirl.
Black holes where the light does fade,
Mysteries in the dark evade.

Comets blaze a transient light,
Witnesses to the ancient night.
Planets carve their patient way,
Stories of another day.

Constellations mark the lore,
Heroes, truths, and legends, more.
Written in the stars so bright,
Chapters of eternal night.

Each a tale of untold lore,
Boundless skies and so much more.
In the cosmos, we reside,
Chronicles in stars, worldwide.

Starry Serenades

Underneath the night's embrace,
Stars begin their soft grace.
Whispering through cosmic winds,
Melodies that never end.

Each star sings a gentle tune,
Illuminating the velvet moon.
Serenades so wild and free,
Echoes of the galaxy.

Planets hum in silent chords,
Drifting in their mute accords.
Satellites in graceful arcs,
Joining in the starry sparks.

Light-years speak in symphony,
Songs of ancient history.
Rhythms of the universe,
Timeless verses so diverse.

Starry serenades so clear,
Heard by those who choose to hear.
In the night sky's vast expanse,
A celestial, timeless dance.

Wandering Worlds

Beneath the silent, starlit sky
The planets dance, they wander by
Through cosmic seas, they drift and sway
In endless night, where shadows lay

Mysteries in dark expanse
Concealing worlds in timeless trance
Galactic winds their course decide
Orbits twist, and paths collide

Through nebulae, their voyage you trace
A cosmic ballet in endless space
Invisible threads of gravity
Bind wandering worlds in unity

Meteor trails in icy wake
Comets blazing, stars they shake
From dawn 'til dusk of universe
Their journeys etched in verse

Each planet's song, a story told
In whispers ancient, brave, and bold
In wandering worlds, the secrets lie
Of where we come and years gone by

Stellar Peace

Beneath the cloak of twilight deep
The stars upon their vigil keep
Whispers of peace in silent light
Illuminate the boundless night

Soft glimmers of eternity
Shine over lands, beneath the sea
Celestial dreams in tranquil flight
Merge into one harmonious night

Silent symphony in the skies
Echoes of time, clear in our eyes
A galaxy's serene embrace
Reflects upon the human race

Cradled by endless, peace-filled space
We find solitude, gentle grace
In stellar peace, our souls align
With the infinite, the divine

Constellations in hushed glory
Narrate an eternal story
In their glow, we find our place
Amidst the stars, in boundless space

Galaxies' Grace

In endless night, where galaxies bloom
Their radiant light dispels the gloom
Through spiral arms, their beauty soars
A dance of time, forevermore

Majestic streams of starlit beams
Weave through cosmos like ancient dreams
Galaxies grace the heavens wide
In this vast sea, no place to hide

From distant points in spacetime's flow
Their luminous patterns always grow
Interwoven paths, a grand design
Each galaxy, a cosmic shrine

Swirling out in perfect form
Beyond the reach of any storm
In galaxies' grace, we see anew
Infinite, yet ever true

Through telescopes, their light we seek
Patterns vast, symbols unique
Eternal artistry displayed
Galaxies' grace, timelessly portrayed

Astronomical Auras

Auroras blend, celestial paints
Brush the skies in sacred haste
Colors vivid, swirling streams
Woven through our midnight dreams

Stars cast halos, midnight's glow
Wonders deep, above, below
Auroras dance in tranquil space
An astronomical embrace

Mystic lights in rhythm sway
Across the night, this grand ballet
Luminous shades of wondrous hue
Awash in cosmic morning dew

Nebulas pulse in silent shroud
Enchanting every drifting cloud
Through auras bright, we come to see
The boundless scope of all that be

Celestial wings, in flight unfurled
Embrace the curves of our world
In astronomical displays
Our hearts and minds forever praise

Spiral Arm Secrets

In the vaults of night they turn,
Galaxies in a cosmic waltz.
Stars ignite and quietly burn,
Whispers echo in the void's halls.

Light-years pass in silent dance,
Mysteries of distant, gleaming charm.
Ancient rings in a twilight trance,
Reveal the spiral arm's secret balm.

Celestial tales in spectral glow,
Nebulae weave stories untold.
Through starry arches, secrets flow,
In cosmic scripts of endless gold.

Gravity's pull, a delicate sway,
Drawing lines in the interstellar.
Darkness cloaks the night's array,
While stars craft tales that compel her.

Seek the secrets in the stars,
Borne on winds of cosmic flights.
In those arms, across the bars,
Lie the truths of boundless nights.

Dark Matter Musings

Invisible threads in boundless space,
Weaving through the galaxy's form.
Unseen forces setting the pace,
Silent dance in celestial storm.

Beneath the stars, mysteries hide,
In the shadowed depths they cling.
Dark matter's whispering sigh,
To the cosmos, secrets bring.

Gravitational hints align,
In the darkness, shapes defined.
Unknown realms where shadows shine,
Answers shrouded and confined.

Science peers into the dark,
Seeking what the night obscures.
Within the voids, a hidden spark,
That cosmological lore ensures.

Our universe, a vast expanse,
Bound by threads of unseen art.
In dark matter's twilight dance,
Lies the key to every start.

Twinkling Testament

Each star a witness to the past,
A distant light that brightly gleams.
In the sky, their truths amassed,
Reflecting worlds and ancient dreams.

Constellations sketch the tale,
Of cosmic epochs, spread so far.
In their glow, the night unveils,
The testament of each star.

Luminescence through the years,
Piercing through the void's cold air.
In their sparkle, hopes and fears,
Written in their twinkling glare.

Galactic realms in constant flux,
Twisting through the planes unseen.
Stars align in spectral flux,
Painting past in silver sheen.

To gaze upon the night above,
Is to read the universe in time.
A testament to endless love,
And the poetry of the divine.

Aurora's Allure

In the frost of polar night,
Aurora dances in the sky.
Curtains weave in ghostly light,
Colors swirling, drifting high.

Solar whispers kiss the poles,
Magnetized in vibrant streams.
Aurora's allure gently unfolds,
Crafting ethereal dreams.

Electric hues in jeweled array,
Paint the night in splendid hues.
Nature's canvas on display,
In shades of green and blues.

Through the silence, visions gleam,
A symphony in drifting light.
Magic weaves a transient dream,
In the tapestry of night.

Lost in fire's gentle sway,
Mesmerized by night's allure.
Aurora's dance at close of day,
A memory forever pure.

Milky Way Musings

In the heart of the sky's embrace,
A river of stars does trace,
Whispers of time and space,
Eternal, in their dance of grace.

Galactic arms in a sacred twirl,
Around the cosmic swirl,
Dreams from eons unfurl,
A luminous, silvery pearl.

Constellations draw the lore,
In patterns ancient, soar,
As light beams from before,
Tell tales of forevermore.

Silent, the astral choir sings,
On celestial, fleeting wings,
As night its velvet brings,
And unto the cosmos clings.

Nebula Nights

A swirl of colors bright,
In nebula's tender light,
Cosmic dust taking flight,
In the deep, silent night.

Stars are born in a haze,
In the heavens' vast maze,
A creation's gentle phrase,
Set in the void to blaze.

Nebula veils the dark,
Embroidered by starlight spark,
A cosmic playground mark,
In endless, boundless arc.

Whisper to the night so wide,
In nebula where dreams collide,
Secrets in the stars we bide,
Guided by the universe's tide.

Venus's Veil

Amidst the evening's embrace,
Shines Venus with tender grace,
In the twilight's mystic space,
Enigmatic, face to face.

Beneath her marbled shroud,
Lies a realm ever proud,
Of volcanic peaks and cloud,
In mysteries softly bowed.

Shepherdess of love and light,
Glows in the velvet night,
Her veil a silent sight,
In dawn's embrace, takes flight.

Beauty in the heavens high,
Adorns the cosmic sky,
Venus, a silken sigh,
On which our dreams rely.

Spectral Horizons

On horizons spectral bend,
Where light and dark transcend,
Stars and shadows blend,
And colours apprehend.

Dawn breaks on the astral sea,
In a dance of light set free,
Infinite hues decree,
An eternal, astral spree.

Galaxies in horizon's reach,
A cosmic lesson to teach,
In silence do beseech,
The secrets of the breach.

Across the spectral glow,
The cosmos ebb and flow,
In endless nights bestow,
A radiant, celestial show.

Interstellar Odyssey

Across the void, we sail so wide,
Where cosmic waves and stardust ride.
Galaxies whisper, secrets unfurled,
In the vast expanse of untamed world.

Nebulae glow with brilliant light,
Guiding ships through endless night.
Uncharted realms where dreams do meet,
In silent dance, the stars we greet.

Asteroids drift in silent flight,
Jewels that glisten in the night.
Eternal trek through space so grand,
Beyond the realms of mortal hand.

Through wormholes vast and black holes deep,
Where mysteries in silence sleep.
The universe, an endless sea,
Beckons with its enigma, wild and free.

We journey far, no end in sight,
Through realms of dark and realms of light.
An odyssey through starry beams,
Beyond the stretch of waking dreams.

Eternal Constellations

In the heavens, patterns weave,
Tales of old, we still believe.
Heroes, monsters, lovers' plight,
Written in the starry night.

Orion's belt and Pegasus's flight,
Shine with stories in the night.
Myths of gods and epic fights,
Etched in celestial lights.

From Cassiopeia's regal throne,
To Draco's winding form unknown.
Eternal beacons, guiding true,
In midnight's vast and endless blue.

Ursa Major, proud and grand,
Points the way to northern land.
Unchanging through the aeons, vast,
Stories from our ancient past.

Constellations ever bright,
Whispering through the endless night.
In their glow, we find our place,
A timeless map of cosmic grace.

Milky Way Wonders

A silken ribbon, skyward bound,
Where marvels of the night are found.
Starry clusters, light so pure,
Milky Way's eternal lure.

Glistening fields of astral bloom,
Illuminate the night's dark gloom.
Navigators' guiding light,
Through the heavens, silvery white.

Nebulae like painted dreams,
In their heart, creation beams.
Stars born in their tender care,
Lighting up the cosmic air.

Galactic arms in spirals vast,
Embrace the future, hold the past.
From Andromeda to our home,
Through the universe, we roam.

Milky Way, with wondrous grace,
A beacon in the cosmic space.
Whisper tales from distant shores,
A galaxy where life explores.

Heavenly Harmonies

In the silent vast expanse,
Where stars and planets spin and dance,
A symphony of light and tone,
In the cosmos, we are not alone.

Nebulae sing with vibrant hue,
Galaxies twist in splendid view.
The music of the spheres so grand,
Resonate across the land.

Celestial bodies in their flight,
Compose a melody of light.
Eternal tunes that never cease,
A cosmic song of hope and peace.

From supernovae's brilliant blast,
To comets on their journeys vast.
Every note, a story told,
In harmonies both brave and bold.

Listen close, the heavens speak,
In tones so vast, yet soft and meek.
A cosmic choir, eternally,
Sings the song of you and me.

Orbiting Reveries

Around the stars, my thoughts do twirl,
In cosmic dance, a dream unfurled,
Through stardust paths, my visions sway,
In night's embrace, they softly play.

Celestial winds, they guide my soul,
Towards a distant, shining goal,
In orbits vast, my heart does glide,
On waves of light, I gently ride.

Nebulous whispers kiss my mind,
Leaving earthly cares behind,
In realms where only dreams can soar,
I'm bound to wander evermore.

Galaxies echo endless tunes,
Beneath the watchful, silver moons,
In every star's resplendent gleam,
I find the heart of every dream.

Thus in this endless, starry sprawl,
Where quiet shadows softly fall,
My orbiting reveries dwell,
In cosmic tides, they rise and swell.

Dawning Nebulae

As dawn within the void appears,
In cosmic dance, devoid of fears,
Nebulae paint the sky so wide,
In colors mixed with morning's tide.

A birth of stars in swirling hues,
Their infant light in bloom bestrews,
The heavens watch with ancient eyes,
As new day's whispers softly rise.

In twilight's grasp, they gently glow,
Their luminous hearts begin to show,
An astral bloom of light's array,
To greet the birth of a new day.

Beneath this sky in waking sigh,
Nebulae weave dreams gone by,
Their woven light a tale unfolds,
Of time and space in endless holds.

In each new dawn, a promise wakes,
Of wonders born as darkness breaks,
And through the cosmic veil displayed,
Rise new nebulae, unafraid.

Galactic Glimmer

Upon the void, a shimmer bright,
Galactic glitters, vast delight,
In skies of velvet, softly spun,
A billion hearts beat as one.

Each speck of light, a timeless tale,
Of cosmic winds and stellar gale,
In nights of dark, they brightly gleam,
Illuminating realms of dream.

Wreathed in the dust of ancient stars,
We wander 'neath their glistening bars,
In orbits long and pathways grand,
They guide us through the endless span.

With every twinkle, whispers draw,
Us closer to the cosmic awe,
In every glint a secret lies,
Of worlds unseen by waking eyes.

And so we gaze with open hearts,
At celestial art that night imparts,
In glimmering bounds our spirits fly,
Amid the tapestry of the sky.

Astral Annotations

Upon the starry scroll of night,
In silver script through endless flight,
Astral tales are softly penned,
In celestial ink, they never end.

Each constellation, drawn so clear,
Whispers legends we hold dear,
A cosmic chronicle, bright and bold,
In every star a story told.

Nebulae, in hues profound,
Offer notes in silence found,
Their vibrant lights and shadowed dance,
Write sagas of the endless expanse.

The moon, a silvered scribe on high,
Inscribes her prose upon the sky,
With every phase and tender glow,
She marks the passage of time's flow.

Thus in the night, with eyes alight,
We read the tales of boundless height,
In every spark, an echo rings,
Of the universe and all its things.

Quantum Quests

In realms unseen, the particles dance,
A mystic waltz in cosmic expanse.
Threads of time, intricately spun,
Quantum quests, where all is one.

Waves collapse and realms unfurl,
Dimensions twist in cosmic whirl.
Secrets lie in twilight's grasp,
Futures meld with the past.

Entangled fates in photons we find,
Woven stories of the cosmic mind.
Matter and energy, a cryptic spree,
In the quantum dreams of eternity.

Parallel worlds in silent flight,
Merge and part in the darkened night.
Through the void, whispers crest,
In a quantum journey's quest.

Stars align in a delicate trance,
Particles glow in spectral dance.
Infinite paths where choices rest,
On the quantum quest's finest test.

Crimson Constellations

Night's embrace, the heavens bloom,
Crimson hues in cosmic plume.
Stars ignite in a ruby sky,
Crimson constellations fly.

Whispers echo in velvet space,
Galaxies burn in tender grace.
Nebulae paint the astral sea,
In crimson's ancient decree.

Celestial fires in crimson tide,
Eternal dance the stars abide.
Through the void, colors surge,
On crimson trails, their spirits merge.

Galactic whispers, a silent song,
In constellations, they belong.
Ruby lights and silent gleams,
Guide us through our dreams.

In scarlet realms, the night recalls,
Celestial lores in mystic halls.
Crimson constellations glow,
In the silent cosmic flow.

Orbital Overtures

Planets spin in a grand ballet,
Celestial arcs in night's display.
Orbital paths trace a silent tune,
In the light of a distant moon.

Stardust swirls in twilight's hold,
Tales of time in whispers told.
Solar winds in subtle flight,
Sing the overtures of night.

Comets blaze in transient arcs,
In the void, they leave their marks.
Orbital dances, ancient and vast,
Songs of futures and of past.

Rings of ice in Saturn's thrall,
Distant echoes in their call.
Points of light through cosmos strewn,
Orbital overtures attune.

Majestic spheres in constant spin,
Orchestras of the stars begin.
Orbital paths in grand allure,
Sing their timeless overture.

Zenith's Zephyr

High above where eagles soar,
Zephyr breathes forevermore.
At the zenith of the sky,
Wind and stars in harmony fly.

Whispers ride the azure breeze,
Through the canopy of trees.
Zenith's peak, a tranquil crest,
In the zephyr's gentle rest.

Skies embrace the endless flight,
Clouds merge in soft twilight.
Spirits drift in serene shores,
As zeal within the wind implores.

Mountains kiss the sky so clear,
Held by zephyrs ever near.
In the zenith's lullaby,
Dreams ascend and never die.

Zephyr's touch in golden hue,
At the zenith, life renews.
Infinite paths where spirits fly,
On the zephyr's gentle sigh.

Tales of the Universe

In the silence of night, the cosmos sings
A melody ancient, each star it brings
Planets whisper secrets of times untold
Galaxies dance, their stories unfold

Nebulae cradle, the starry birth
Comets streak across celestial girth
Voices of void hum a cosmic tune
Lit by the glow of a silver moon

Dark matter hides in the shadows deep
Guarding the tales the black holes keep
Meteor showers paint skies with grace
As asteroids chart their endless chase

Orion hunts with his belt so bright
Guiding sailors through the boundless night
The universe murmurs, a lullaby
Rocking the cradle of time gone by

Moonbeams filter through cosmic haze
Illuminating the Milky Way's maze
Tales of the universe, vast and grand
Whispered by starlight, hand in hand

Distant Luminaries

Far above the earthly clamor
Stars ignite in a celestial glamour
Astral flames in the canvas black
Lighting paths we cannot track

From galaxies distant and far-flung
Their radiant songs are softly sung
Echoes of light, both old and new
In cosmic chorus, they shine through

Quasars blaze with untamed fire
Pulsars pulse with rhythmic desire
Each photon carries a tale and dream
A silent shout, a brilliant beam

Binary stars in eternal dance
Glimmering through the vast expanse
Novae burst in glorious might
Shattered remnants, a dazzling sight

In the velvety void they draw their course
Guiding the traveler without remorse
Distant luminaries, fierce and bold
Their light, an ancient story told

Constellation Conversations

Whispering winds through the cosmic sea
Speak the language of eternity
Constellations chat in silent tones
Mapping histories with celestial stones

Leo roars with a lion's pride
Cancer's claws reaching far and wide
Pisces swims in the starry night
Aquarius pours with serene delight

Andromeda waits, a distant throne
Echoes of myths in her twilight zone
Cassiopeia's throne, a crooked seat
As Perseus flies with wings on his feet

Ursa Major guides with steady hand
While Ursa Minor guards Polaris land
Gemini twins converse through light
Their cosmic bond, forever tight

Through the ages these patterns remain
Stars conversing in a stellar domain
Constellation conversations in the skies
Endless chatter, in light they rise

Night Sky Narratives

Under the dome of the twilight hue
Stars weave the tales both old and new
Galactic stories in silver streams
Telling the dozers their cosmic dreams

The night sky hums in whispered prose
Orion's prowess, the Pleiades' pose
Scorpio's sting and Draco's flight
Threads of legends, they dance in night

Aurora paints with ethereal brush
Northern lights in a vibrant rush
Ghostly veils, the heavens share
Their transient art, divinely fair

Starlit handwrites on midnight's loom
Patterns of old, in the starry gloom
Seafarer's guides and lover's signs
Interwoven by fate's design

Night sky narratives, timeless lore
Written in light from far off shore
Through infinite space their stories glide
Foretelling tales the universe confide

Midnight Mirage

Under the velvet sky, dreams arise,
Midnight whispers secrets wise,
Stars blink tales from afar,
Night's canvas paints the power of char.

Desert sands glow under lunar light,
Horizon blurs in the softest sight,
Winds carry murmurs of night's shroud,
Mirage entwines, dreams unbowed.

Oasis gleams in the moonbeams' cast,
Reflections of time in shadows vast,
Silent steps through silver dunes,
Mirage dances to ethereal tunes.

Whispers of night in stillness reside,
Mystic waves in a cosmic glide,
Midnight's allure, a phantom embrace,
Dreams dissolve in a tranquil space.

Invisible threads weave night's attire,
Guardian stars in celestial choir,
Echoes of dreams in silence surge,
Midnight's mirage, a mystic urge.

Infinite Orbits

Around the cosmic dance, they move,
In spirals of time, they groove,
Celestial spheres in endless flight,
Trace the patterns in the night.

Eclipsing paths of shadowed grace,
Planets' waltz in vast space,
Cycle's rhythm, an eternal art,
Infinity's dance, where dreams start.

Galaxies spin in a radiant ballet,
Nebulous curtains in grand array,
Stars align in harmonic trance,
Infinite orbits in cosmic romance.

Above the ether, poised and grand,
Celestial choreography, hand in hand,
Celestial whispers in silent mime,
Orbits speak of endless time.

Constellations in rhythmic sway,
Tracing skylines, night and day,
Infinite orbits, a timeless quest,
Universe in harmony, forever blessed.

Sapphire Spheres

In the deep abyss, they glow,
Sapphire spheres in twilight's show,
Reflecting oceans, skies so blue,
In a silent world, they whisper true.

Water's embrace, so gentle and strong,
Echoes of creation, an ageless song,
Hidden depths in sapphire's gleam,
Worlds within in a lucid dream.

Crystalline waters in tranquil grace,
Holding secrets in their embrace,
Spheres of sapphire, deep and wide,
Where mysteries of the heart reside.

Beneath the waves, in quiet repose,
Life's tapestry, gently flows,
Sapphire hues in the ocean's breath,
Whispers of life, beyond death.

Blue horizons in every tear,
Spheres that hold, every fear,
Sapphire worlds in timeless streams,
Mirrors of dreams, in blue beams.

Stellar Silences

In the stillness of the night,
Stellar silences take flight,
Whispers of stars, soft and bright,
Echo through the endless height.

Silhouettes against the dark,
Stars etch stories, leave a mark,
Cosmic quiet in vast expanse,
Stellar silences in celestial dance.

Each twinkle holds a secret close,
Mysteries of time in silent pose,
Galactic whispers, soft and clear,
In the silence, stars appear.

Nebulae in silence bloom,
In the cosmic quiet, there's room,
For whispers of the universe,
Stellar silences, a soft verse.

Light-years away in tranquil space,
Stellar silences in cosmic grace,
In the stillness, universe unfurls,
Where silence speaks and darkness twirls.

Galactic Whispers

Stars resonate in the midnight's glow,
Silent tales they softly bestow.
Infinite secrets in cosmic veils,
Mysteries told through celestial trails.

Planets align in a symphonic dance,
Spirals of time in a timeless trance.
Galaxies murmur of epochs long past,
Universal stories meant to last.

Constellations weave ancient lore,
Shapes of myths from times of yore.
Whispers of light travel so far,
Messages sent from a distant star.

Meteor showers paint the night,
Fragments of dreams in transient flight.
Across the void, they glide and sing,
Whispers of hope on a cosmic string.

Black holes hum their solemn tone,
Echoing secrets never known.
In the silence of the vast expanse,
Galactic whispers tell their trance.

Moonlit Murmurs

Underneath the silvery moon,
Whispers drift in a lullabied tune.
Waves of night caress the shore,
Dreams unlocked in the twilight's door.

Luminous beams through leaves doth creep,
Casting shadows where secrets sleep.
Owls hoot in a gentle song,
Moonlit murmurs echo long.

Winds of the night share ancient tales,
Songs of love in whispering gales.
Cicadas hum in harmony,
A symphony through the canopy.

Softly glows the night's embrace,
Starlit dreams in open space.
Midnight whispers flutter away,
Promises of a new day.

The moon looks down in soft caress,
Lighting the world in sheer finesse.
In her gaze, night's voices drift,
Moonlit murmurs a quiet gift.

Cosmic Revelations

In the quiet of the endless night,
Truths emerge in streams of light.
Stars align to speak their mind,
Revelations of the universe, intertwined.

Nebulas pulse in vibrant hues,
Secrets concealed in cosmic clues.
Shooting stars their knowledge cast,
Truths revealed from the distant past.

Planets whisper as they turn,
Ancient stories they discern.
Through the void, a silent teach,
Cosmic wisdom within reach.

Galaxies twist in spiral veins,
Knowledge hidden in their chains.
Light traverses space's sea,
Revelations of infinity.

Black hole's gravity does call,
Unveiling truths within their thrall.
In the stillness of the night,
Cosmic revelations ignite.

Nebula's Embrace

Through the void, nebula sways,
Colors burst in vibrant arrays.
Dust and gas in a cosmic dance,
In the vastness, they entrance.

Stardust forms in tender hold,
New worlds born from stories old.
Within the nebulous caress,
Creation's artistry, nothing less.

Galactic winds whisper low,
Through the stars they softly blow.
In the cradle of space's grace,
Embraced by the nebula's face.

Darkness meets the light's glow,
Mysteries in their beauty flow.
Infinity in every trace,
Wonder in the nebula's embrace.

Stars emerge from the ethereal fog,
Life begins in cosmic dialogue.
In the heart of space's lace,
Nurtured by the nebula's embrace.

Orbiting Desires

In the dance of celestial fire
Hearts revolve, enraptured, drawn
Gravity binds each silent quire
In twilight's grip, till night is gone

Through endless dark, incessant spin
Faint whispers echo, sparks alight
Love's orbit pulls us deep within
Dreams ignited by the night

Starlit passions, magnet flows
Cosmic tides of longing sway
Endless journey where shadows glow
We lose ourselves in heavens' play

Ecliptic paths our souls entwine
Infinite embrace, forlorn
In cosmic field, our fates align
Love reborn, celestial morn

In void's vast reach, desires burn
Endlessly, our hearts ignite
In orbit's pull, we soon return
To find solace in starlit night

Planetary Paths

Upon the trail of ancient days
Wisdom carved in stellar stone
Through cosmic winds and solar rays
The path unknown, our spirits flown

Beneath the arch of milky streams
Mysteries etched in light and dark
Planets dance in silent dreams
Stamping time with every mark

Orbit's course, a guiding thread
Round the sun, orbits weave
Interstellar tales are read
In whispers that the stars believe

Through void and stretch of empty night
An endless pilgrimage, we wend
Planetary paths alight
On trails of stardust, we ascend

In fated arcs, our lives align
With cosmic beats our hearts confide
Upon this journey, love defines
In planetary paths, beside

Supernova Sentiments

In the heart of darkness deep
A blaze of light ignites the sky
Stars are born from night where sleep
Celestial tears, our spirits cry

Supernova bright, we shine
Explosions of our quests and dreams
Fragmented shards of joy, divine
Painted in the cosmic streams

Sentiments of stars ablaze
Tell stories of the ages passed
From scattered light in heaven's maze
Eternity within us, cast

Nebulous whispers call our name
In stellar winds of fate, we soar
Emotions burning, endless flame
Supernova's heart we explore

The cosmic lullaby will sing
Of supernova's fleeting might
Through stardust fields, our love will cling
In sentiments of eternal light

Beyond the Horizon

Gaze upon the edge of sight
Where sky and earth converge as one
A realm beyond the day and night
Whispers of the stars begun

Beyond the horizon, dreams do wait
Carried by the wind, they soar
In twilight's grasp, we contemplate
The mysteries on distant shore

To far off realms our hearts are bound
Where sun and moon your wishes guide
Horizon's veil, where love is found
Forever whispers on the tide

In twilight's glow, the path is clear
A journey to the great unknown
Past horizon's edge, no fear
In love's embrace, forever blown

Beyond the horizon, futures gleam
In starlit glow, our fates entwine
Eternal light in endless dream
Horizon's truth, in hearts, define

Milton Keynes UK
Ingram Content Group UK Ltd.
UKHW022004310524
443378UK00014B/631

9 789916 399637